Twice as Good

By RICHARD MICHELSON

Illustrated by ERIC VELASQUEZ

THE STORY OF WILLIAM POWELL AND CLEARVIEW, THE ONLY GOLF COURSE
DESIGNED, BUILT, AND OWNED BY AN AFRICAN AMERICAN

Willie Powell was fast.

He was only in third grade, and he could run across the
playground faster than most fifth graders. But the new golf
course was seven miles outside of town, and he'd promised
his mother he would be home before dark.

Edgewater Golf Course was the most beautiful sight Willie's eyes had ever seen. The lawns were as smooth as carpets.

Willie approached two golfers. "Can you teach me to play?" he asked the kinder looking of the men.

"Son, didn't anyone ever tell you that your kind is not welcome here?" the man answered.

Willie's eyes wanted to cry, but he wouldn't let them. Of course, Willie knew he was different. He was the only Negro in his class.

❖

It was dark when Willie got home.

He hoped his mother would be asleep, but she was waiting by the door. First she hugged Willie tight. And then she told him, "Now you go get me a good whippy switch from one of the willows."

Willie knew he deserved a switchin', but even now he was planning to sneak back to the new golf course every chance he got. Getting in trouble wasn't going to stop Willie.

"You back again, son?" It was the same man who'd mocked Willie weeks before. "You may as well learn to caddy. That means you can carry my clubs." He handed Willie a leather bag filled with fourteen sticks carved from thick hickory wood. It was heavy, but Willie already knew he'd have to work twice as hard as the other caddies.

His school principal had told him, "If you are going to get ahead in this world, Willie, you can't be as good as the white children; you have to be twice as good."

By the following year Willie was being paid 35 cents per bag to caddy. He liked jingling the money in his pocket. He'd caddy every summer day and study how the better players hit the ball. Then he'd hike to Dr. Casey's house, where his mother worked answering the phone and writing down the doctor's appointments.

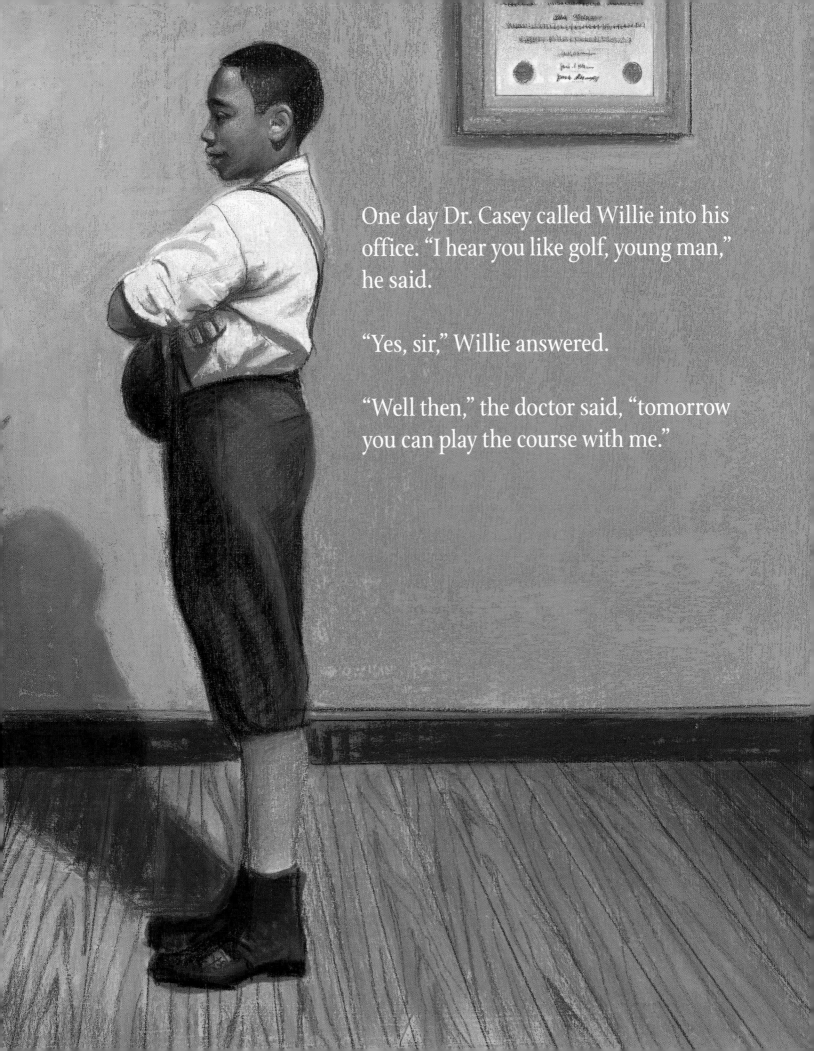

One day Dr. Casey called Willie into his office. "I hear you like golf, young man," he said.

"Yes, sir," Willie answered.

"Well then," the doctor said, "tomorrow you can play the course with me."

Willie woke up before the sun and raced the whole way to Edgewater. When he saw Dr. Casey's car, he hurried over and swung the doctor's golf bag over his shoulder. "I asked you to play, young man, not to caddy," Dr. Casey said, and he handed Willie his very own set of clubs.

Willie knew it was rare for a white man to help a colored child, but he couldn't think of a single word to say. Finally, Willie just set his ball on the first tee and took a swing. The ball rose like a shooting star, high into the sky.

Willie practiced every chance he got. By the time he entered Minerva High he was the best golfer in the school. Willie was proud to be named team captain, and he was sure that if he got a chance to compete, he could even win the local junior tournament. So one morning, Willie hitchhiked twenty-one miles to Orchard Hills.

The judges never expected a Negro to enter the competition, so they hadn't forbidden it in the rules. Willie had caddied for many Orchard Hills' members and they all liked him. But now they looked away.

"Let the boy play," he finally heard one of the men say. It was the man he'd first caddied for years before.

Willie's hands started to sweat. He was so nervous he could barely hold the club. But he took a deep breath and walked to the first tee.

By the time he got to the fifteenth fairway, Willie was leading the field and it seemed like the whole town was watching. His next drive was heading straight for the pin. But on the way down, his ball nicked the skinniest twig hanging off of a huge maple, and came to rest in the knee-high grass.

"That'll teach his kind to play on our course," he heard someone say.

Willie finished third but he didn't give up. "I'll just have to work twice as hard the next time," he promised himself.

And Willie did keep working hard. He went to college, married his sweetheart, Marcella, and went looking for a steady factory job. But America was at war, and soon Willie was drafted into the army.

Willie put on his uniform and hugged Marcella goodbye. He was Sergeant William Powell now, and he had to sail across the ocean to England.

❖

Sometimes Willie had to work all day and night at the army base. But whenever he had time off, Willie would play golf. It seemed like every town in England had a course. The local people were always polite. Nobody seemed to think golf was a game for *whites only*. Willie had never enjoyed golfing more, but after three years away, he was thankful when the war was finally over. He missed Marcella and couldn't wait to sail home.

Willie was glad to be back in America, and best of all, Marcella was soon pregnant. She had been dreaming about having a daughter. Willie had been dreaming, too. His dream was to be a professional golfer, and his welcome overseas made him think it was possible.

But Willie heard the same story at every course he visited that year. "Only members are allowed to play here, and you're a little old to caddy, son."

"Some folks don't mind me fighting for their freedom," he told Marcella, "but they sure do mind me sharing their clubhouse."

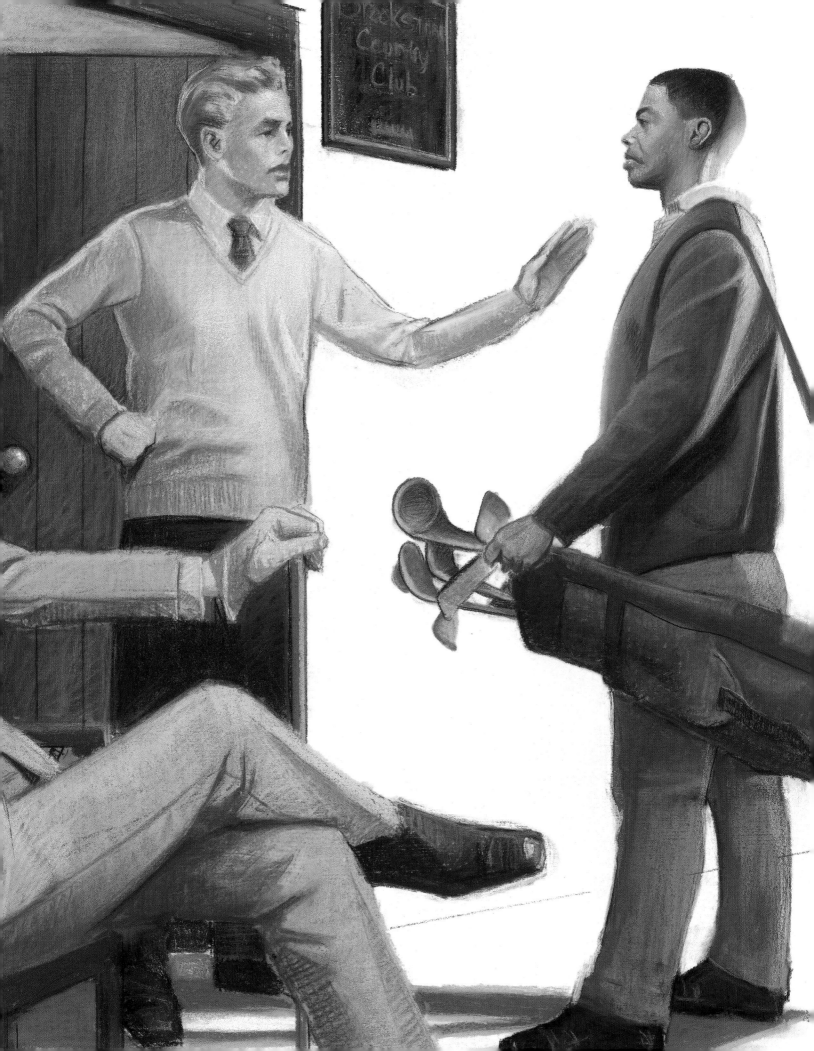

But today, nothing could upset Willie. He was playing with his baby daughter Renee. She grabbed his finger and held it tight.

"You have the grip of a champion golfer," he told her.

Marcella laughed. "But Renee's a girl," she reminded Willie.

"I know she's a *girl*," Willie answered. "She'll just have to try twice as hard as the boys do."

"And she's colored," Marcella said.

"I know she's *colored*," Willie answered. "She'll just have to try twice as hard as the white folks do."

Then Willie gave Renee a big kiss and held her up high.

"Someday there will be a course where you'll never be turned away," he told her.

The next afternoon Willie and Marcella were driving past their favorite farmland when they saw a wooden sign. Willie stopped the car and got out. He strolled right past the chicken coops, the milking barns, the silos, and even the sweet potato patch. There were rolling hills and he had a *clear view* in every direction. "From right here," he told himself, "I can see clear into the future."

Willie knew the government was lending former soldiers money, called GI loans, to help them buy homes. So he went to the local bank where his friends had received these loans. But the bankers had never expected a Negro to ask for money. They all liked Willie, but now they looked away.

Willie wouldn't give up. He'd just have to try twice as hard to raise the money. He finally convinced two local colored doctors to help him buy the land.

For two years Willie worked at the local factory from three in the afternoon until eleven at night to support his family. At the first crack of dawn, he'd head out to dig, weed, mow, plant, and water. He'd work until it was time to leave again for the factory. The harder Willie worked, the better he felt.

"Your daddy is putting 'the fair back in fairway'" Marcella told Renee. "He is a groundbreaker and you'll be one, too." Then she laughed because Willie was out digging in the ground again. What she'd meant was that William Powell was ahead of his time.

In April 1948, Clearview Golf Club was ready to open.

"This course for coloreds only or can I play, too?" someone shouted from the road. Willie recognized the man he had caddied for when he was nine years old.

"This is America's course," Willie answered proudly. "The only color that matters here is the color of the greens."

Clearview had been open one year, and Renee was turning three years old when Willie gave her a small golf club for her birthday. It fit perfectly in her tiny hands.

As Renee grew up she didn't care that some folks thought Negroes shouldn't be allowed to play golf. And she didn't care that some folks thought girls shouldn't be allowed to play golf. Renee fell in love with the game.

❖

"Come in for dinner," Marcella called.

"I'm not done practicing," Renee answered. "I need to try twice as hard if I am going to be a champion."

Willie gave his daughter a big hug. "You already are *my* champion," he told her.

Renee hugged her daddy back. She felt twice as good as she had ever felt before.

The Rest of the Story

Renee Powell kept practicing, and in 1963, at age 16, she became the first African American to play in the United States Girls' Junior Championship, one year and eight days before Martin Luther King Jr.'s "I Have a Dream" speech.

In 1995 the Renee Powell Youth Camp Program was launched, giving inner city kids of all backgrounds and nationalities, opportunities to play the game of golf and the following year Renee became the first African American female Class A member of the PGA. She was also named as a consultant to the First Tee Program, whose aim is to teach children the joy of golf and its lessons in integrity and other positive behavior skills. Renee currently serves as the head golf professional at Clearview Golf Course and her younger brother Lawrence is the course superintendent. In 2001 the Clearview Legacy Foundation was established as a tax exempt charitable foundation to preserve the course for future generations, and to honor the history of "America's Course."

When William Powell started building Clearview Golf Course by hand in 1946, professional sports were still segregated. Jackie Robinson wouldn't integrate major league baseball until the following year. Until 1961, the PGA of America had a "Caucasian only" clause, and William Powell was denied membership because of his race. He was inducted into the National Black Golf Hall of Fame in 1996 and in 1998 was awarded a retroactive lifetime PGA membership. In 2009, at age 92, months before his death, Powell received the PGA Distinguished Service Award, the association's highest honor.

Today, Clearview is not only a National Historic Site, but it also stands as a monument symbolizing what one individual can achieve against incredible odds and obstacles.

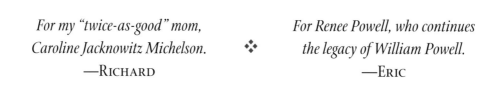

For my "twice-as-good" mom,
Caroline Jacknowitz Michelson.
—RICHARD

❖

For Renee Powell, who continues
the legacy of William Powell.
—ERIC

Sleeping Bear Press™ • Sleeping Bear Press is an imprint of Gale, a part of Cengage Learning • 315 East Eisenhower, Suite 200, Ann Arbor, MI 48108 • www.sleepingbearpress.com • Text Copyright © 2012 Richard Michelson • Illustration Copyright © 2012 Eric Velasquez • All rights reserved. No part of this book may be reproduced in any manner without the express written consent of the publisher, except in the case of brief excerpts in critical reviews and articles. • Printed and bound in China. • 10 9 8 7 6 5 4 3 2 1 • Library of Congress Cataloging-in-Publication Data • Michelson, Richard • Twice as good: the story of William Powell and clearview, the only golf course designed, built and owned by an African-American • written by Richard Michelson • illustrated by Eric Velasquez • p. cm. • ISBN 978-1-58536-466-4 • 1. Powell, William J., 1916- • 2. Golf course architects—United States—Biography • 3. Golf courses—United States—Design and construction—History—Juvenile literature. • 4. African American businesspeople. • 5. Discrimination in sports. • I. Velasquez, Eric. II. Title.• GV964.P69M53 2011 • 796.352092—dc23 • [B] • 2011029114

Printed by China Translation & Printing Services Limited,Guangdong Province,China. 1st printing. 10/2011